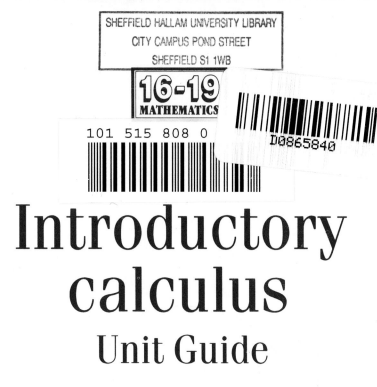

Introductory calculus

Unit Guide

The School Mathematics Project

REFERENCE

CAMBRIDGE
UNIVERSITY PRESS

Main authors

Stan Dolan
Andy Hall
Michael Leach
Timothy Lewis
Richard Peacock
Paul Roder

Jeff Searle
David Tall
Brian Wardle
Thelma Wilson
Phil Wood

Team leader and project director   Stan Dolan

The authors would like to give special thanks to Ann White for her help in producing the trial edition and in preparing this book for publication.

Published by the Press Syndicate of the University of Cambridge
The Pitt Building, Trumpington Street, Cambridge CB2 1RP
40 West 20th Street, New York, NY 10011–4211, USA
10 Stamford Road, Oakleigh, Victoria 3166, Australia

First published 1991
Reprinted 1992

Produced by Gecko Limited, Bicester, Oxon.

Cover design by Iguana Creative Design

Printed in Great Britain at the University Press, Cambridge

British Library cataloguing in publication data
16–19 mathematics.
Introductory calculus
Unit guide
1. Calculus
I. School Mathematics Project
515

ISBN 0 521 40845 8

Contents

Introduction to 16–19 Mathematics

Nobody reads introductions and nobody reads teachers' guides, so what chance does the introduction to this Unit Guide have? The least we can do is to keep it short! We hope that you will find the discussion point and tasksheet commentaries and ideas on presentation and enrichment useful.

The School Mathematics Project was founded in 1961 with the purpose of improving the teaching of mathematics in schools by the provision of new course materials. SMP authors are experienced teachers and each new venture is tested by schools in a draft version before publication. Work on *16–19 Mathematics* started in 1986 and the pilot of the course has been used by over 30 schools since 1987.

Since its inception the SMP has always offered an 'after sales service' for teachers using its materials. If you have any comments on *16–19 Mathematics*, or would like advice on its use, please write to:

16–19 Mathematics
The SMP Office
The University
Southampton SO9 5NH

Why 16–19 Mathematics?

A major problem in mathematics education is how to enable ordinary mortals to comprehend in a few years concepts which geniuses have taken centuries to develop. In theory, our view of how to pass on this body of knowledge effectively and pleasurably has changed considerably; but no great revolution in practice has been seen in sixth-form classrooms generally. We hope that in this course, the change in approach to mathematics teaching embodied in GCSE schemes will be carried forward. The principles applied in the course are appropriate to this aim.

- Students are actively involved in developing mathematical ideas.
- Premature abstraction and over-reliance on algorithms are avoided.
- Wherever possible, problems arise from, or at least relate to, everyday life.
- Appropriate use is made of modern technology such as graphic calculators and microcomputers.
- Misunderstandings are confronted and acted upon.

By applying these principles and presenting material in an attractive way, A level mathematics is made more accessible to students and more meaningful to them as individuals. The *16–19 Mathematics* course is flexible enough to provide for the whole range of students who obtain at least a grade C at GCSE.

Structure of the courses

The A and AS level courses have a core-plus-options structure. Details of the full range of possibilities, including A and AS level *Further Mathematics* courses, may be obtained from the Joint Matriculation Board, Manchester M15 6EU.

For the A level course *Mathematics (Pure with Applications)*, students must study eight core units and a further two optional units. The structure diagram below shows how the units are related to each other. Other optional units are presently being developed to give students an opportunity to study aspects of mathematics which are appropriate to their personal interests and enthusiasms.

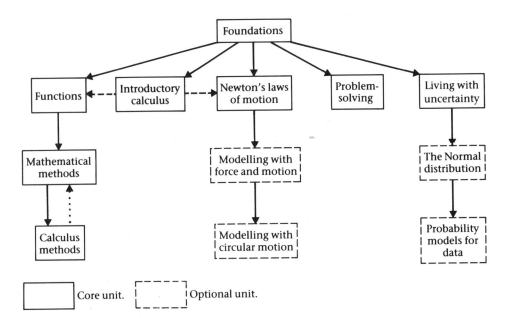

The *Foundations* unit should be started before or at the same time as any other core unit.

Any of the other units can be started at the same time as the *Foundations* unit. The second half of *Functions* requires prior coverage of *Introductory calculus*. *Newton's laws of motion* requires calculus notation which is covered in the initial chapters of *Introductory calculus*.

The Polynomial approximations chapter in *Mathematical methods* requires prior coverage of some sections of *Calculus methods*.

For the AS level *Mathematics (Pure with Applications)* course, students must study *Foundations*, *Introductory calculus* and *Functions*. Students must then study a further two applied units.

Material

In traditional mathematics texts the theory has been written in a didactic manner for passive reading, in the hope that it will be accepted and understood – or, more realistically, that the teacher will supply the necessary motivation and deal with problems of understanding. In marked contrast, *16–19 Mathematics* adopts a questing mode, demanding the active participation of students. The textbooks contain several new devices to aid a more active style of learning.

- Topics are opened up through **group discussion points**, signalled in the text by the symbol

and enclosed in rectangular frames. These consist of pertinent questions to be discussed by students, with guidance and help from the teacher. Commentaries for discussion points are included in this unit guide.

- The text is also punctuated by **thinking points**, having the shape

and again containing questions. These should be dealt with by students without the aid of the teacher. In facing up to the challenge offered by the thinking points it is intended that students will achieve a deeper insight and understanding. A solution within the text confirms or modifies the student's response to each thinking point.

- At appropriate points in the text, students are referred to **tasksheets** which are placed at the end of the relevant chapter. These mostly consist of a self-contained piece of work which is used to investigate a concept prior to any formal exposition. In many cases, it takes up an idea raised in a discussion point, examining it in more detail and preparing the way for formal treatment. There are also **extension tasksheets** (labelled by an E) for higher attaining students which investigate a topic in more depth and **supplementary tasksheets** (labelled by an S) which are intended to help students with a relatively weak background in a particular topic. Commentaries for all the tasksheets are included in this unit guide.

The aim of the **exercises** is to check full understanding of principles and give the student confidence through reinforcement of his or her understanding.

Graphic calculators/microcomputers are used throughout the course. In particular, much use is made of graph plotters. The use of videos and equipment for practical work is also recommended.

As well as the textbooks and unit guides, there is a *Teacher's resource file*. This file contains:

- review sheets which may be used for homework or tests;

- datasheets;

- technology datasheets which give help with using particular calculators or pieces of software;

- a programme of worksheets for more able students which would, in particular, help prepare them for the STEP examination.

Introduction to the unit (for the teacher)

This unit is written as an introduction to calculus. The aim is to develop the concepts of calculus with a greater depth of understanding but at a slower pace than is traditional. Therefore, the unit should also be useful for students who have previously studied calculus techniques without perhaps fully understanding what they have been doing.

The first two chapters cover the differentiation of polynomials. Chapter 3 is concerned with applying the derived function in optimisation problems. This chapter also looks at how calculus aids graph sketching and should be tackled only after completion of chapter 3 from *Foundations*. Chapter 4 covers numerical integration. The final chapter investigates the connection between differentiation and integration and introduces indefinite integrals.

Because concepts are gradually built up it is important that able students do not simply skip to the 'results'. However, there is no need to labour a point once a concept has been thoroughly grasped. For example, a student who can cope easily with tasksheet 3 of chapter 2 should be able to move on rapidly to the use of software as on tasksheet 5.

Using this unit

Much of the material is aimed at different stages in the conceptual development of the subject and intermediate results are often superceded by later results. Students should therefore find this unit a very easy one to review. However, throughout the unit, students are encouraged to develop geometrical and numerical understanding and not simply acquire a knowledge of algebraic 'results'.

Some additional notes on the individual chapters may prove helpful.

Chapter 1

The chapter introduces the notation of differential calculus and reviews the gradient of straight lines. It is important that students should become familiar with the idea that

$$y = au + bv \quad \Rightarrow \quad \frac{dy}{dx} = a\,\frac{du}{dx} + b\,\frac{dv}{dx}$$

in the simple rate of change contexts of this chapter.

Chapter 2

This chapter is concerned with a careful introduction of some of the stages involved in developing the concept of the derived function.

- An understanding of mathematical gradient as an abstraction of gradients in 'real life'.

- A geometrical understanding of zooming-in and local straightness.

- A feel for gradient graphs.

- A knowledge of how to find gradients numerically.

The algebraic limit process is covered in a later unit but this chapter should lay the foundations. Limits do occur, but they are geometrical and numerical rather than algebraic. For both the geometrical and numerical methods there is no way of knowing when you are 'sufficiently close'. Students, and especially the more able ones, should recognise the limitations of this and see the need for a later algebraic treatment of the topic.

Even extremely able students should find it profitable to work through all the different stages of the chapter, but they should be expected to progress more rapidly to the use of sophisticated software rather than spending much time, for example, in using the gradient measurer.

Chapters 3 and 4

These chapters concentrate on differentiation and integration involving only polynomial functions. With the use of graphic calculators and/or computers it is, of course, possible to tackle applications involving more complicated functions, if this is felt to be appropriate.

The way applications are introduced can greatly affect their effectiveness. For example, it is strongly recommended that cup-cake containers should be available in the classroom when tackling the section on maxima and minima in chapter 3.

Chapter 5

Many students will have become aware of the relationship between integration and differentiation before reaching the section on the fundamental theorem of calculus. This section clarifies the relationship and also provides an excellent topic for discussion of rigour in mathematical argument. Students should be fully aware that, whereas the result appears to be true for any differentiable function, the text only gives the outline of a proof for a function whose graph consists of a series of straight line segments.

Tasksheets and resources

Items in *italics* refer to resources not included in the main text.

Equipment/material needed

Gradient measurers

A graph plotter with a zoom facility and with a facility for plotting the gradient graph and the area graph of a function.

The only other essential resources needed to complement the *Introductory calculus* unit are technology datasheets which can be found in the *Teacher's resource file*. This file also contains various optional worksheets and their commentaries together with full guidance on their use.

1 Rates of change

1.1 Introduction

> If the temperature changes by 10 degrees Celsius, what is the change in degrees Fahrenheit? Repeat for temperature changes of 20 and 50 degrees Celsius.
>
> Find the gradient of the line, and explain its significance.
>
> Find an equation expressing F in terms of C and explain the numbers which occur in your equation.

From the graph, temperature changes of 10, 20, 50 degrees Celsius correspond to changes of 18, 36, 90 degrees Fahrenheit.

The gradient is $\frac{72}{40} = 1.8$ (or $\frac{9}{5}$), and it represents the change in degrees Fahrenheit per degree Celsius (i.e. the change in degrees Fahrenheit corresponding to a change of 1 degree Celsius).

Although it cannot be easily read off accurately from the graph, it should be well known that the intercept is 32, the freezing point of water in °F. Hence

$$F = 1.8C + 32$$

1.2 Linear functions

(a) What can be deduced about the equation of a line which has gradient given by $\dfrac{dy}{dx} = 3$?

(b) Using $y = mx + c$, obtain the equation of the line with $\dfrac{dy}{dx} = 3$ passing through (2, 5).

(c) What can be said about the gradient, $\dfrac{dy}{dx}$, of lines with equations such as $y = 4$ or $x = 6$?

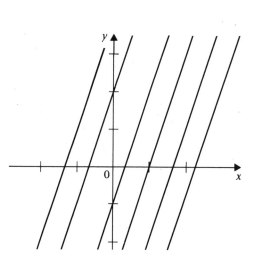

(a) $\dfrac{dy}{dx} = 3$, (i.e. gradient is 3)

$\Rightarrow \quad y = 3x + c$ ①

Because c is not known, any of the lines shown is a possible line; all such lines are said to form the **family** of straight lines with $\dfrac{dy}{dx} = 3$.

(b) In the case in question, (2, 5) is a point on the line. Substituting in ①:

$$5 = 3 \times 2 + c \quad \Rightarrow \quad c = -1$$

So the equation is $y = 3x - 1$.

(c) By choosing two points on the line $y = 4$ as shown, the gradient

$$\frac{dy}{dx} = \frac{0}{4} = 0$$

By choosing any two points on the line $x = 6$, the difference in x-coordinates is shown to be always 0. This leads to division by zero which is not defined. (Refer to *Foundations*, chapter 5, 'Functions'.)

Combined rates of change

1 (a) $v = 20w + 16$ (b) $T = 35w + 46$

  (c) $\dfrac{du}{dw} = 15$, $\dfrac{dv}{dw} = 20$, $\dfrac{dT}{dw} = 35$

    For the first stage, $\dfrac{du}{dw}$ is the change in the time taken in minutes per kilogram of weight (that is, the extra number of minutes needed for an increase in weight of 1 kilogram).

    $\dfrac{dv}{dw}$ and $\dfrac{dT}{dw}$ represent the corresponding changes for the second stage and the overall process.

  (d) For each extra kilogram of weight, the total extra cooking time is the sum of the extra times needed for each of the two stages.

2 $f = 8t$, $s = 200 + 6t$, $x = 200 - 2t$

x represents the distance between the two runners after t seconds.

$$\dfrac{df}{dt} = 8, \qquad \dfrac{ds}{dt} = 6, \qquad \dfrac{dx}{dt} = -2$$

$\dfrac{df}{dt}$ and $\dfrac{ds}{dt}$ are the velocities of the two runners, in $m\,s^{-1}$.

$\dfrac{dx}{dt}$ is the rate of change of the distance between the runners with time, in $m\,s^{-1}$. It is often called the relative velocity. It is negative since this distance is decreasing.

$$\dfrac{dx}{dt} = \dfrac{ds}{dt} - \dfrac{df}{dt}$$

This relation arises since in each second the change in the distance between the two runners will be given by the difference between the distances covered by the runners individually.

TASKSHEET
COMMENTARY

3 (a) $\dfrac{du}{dx} = 3, \qquad \dfrac{dv}{dx} = 2$

(b) (i) $y = (3x + 1) + (2x - 3) \;\Rightarrow\; y = 5x - 2$

(ii) $y = 2(3x + 1) + (2x - 3) \;\Rightarrow\; y = 8x - 1$

(iii) $y = x + 4$ (iv) $y = 6x + 13$

(c) (i) $\dfrac{dy}{dx} = 5$ (ii) $\dfrac{dy}{dx} = 8$ (iii) $\dfrac{dy}{dx} = 1$ (iv) $\dfrac{dy}{dx} = 6$

(d) (i) $\dfrac{dy}{dx} = \dfrac{du}{dx} + \dfrac{dv}{dx}$ (ii) $\dfrac{dy}{dx} = 2\dfrac{du}{dx} + \dfrac{dv}{dx}$

(iii) $\dfrac{dy}{dx} = \dfrac{du}{dx} - \dfrac{dv}{dx}$ (iv) $\dfrac{dy}{dx} = 4\dfrac{du}{dx} - 3\dfrac{dv}{dx}$

(e) The rule should now be apparent. If $y = au + bv$, then

$$\frac{dy}{dx} = a\frac{du}{dx} + b\frac{dv}{dx}$$

(y is called a **linear combination** of u and v.)

4 (a) $u = 12 + 5t$ (b) $v = 9 + 6t$

(c) The first firm is cheaper for jobs lasting longer than 3 hours. The second firm is cheaper for jobs lasting less than 3 hours because of its smaller basic fee.

(d) $\dfrac{du}{dt} = 5$ and $\dfrac{dv}{dt} = 6$ are the two firms' respective extra charges in £ per hour worked.

(e) $c = 3u + 2v$

$$\Rightarrow \frac{dc}{dt} = 3\frac{du}{dt} + 2\frac{dv}{dt} = 27$$

(f) Each extra hour that the job takes costs an extra £27.

2 Gradients of curves

2.1 Locally straight curves

> The diagram shows the positions of four skiers A, B, C and D on a snow-covered hill. Note down some similarities and some differences between the four skiers.

Here are some similarities and differences – you can probably think of others.

- A and D are roughly at the same altitude.

- A is at a peak; B, C and D are on slopes.

- Skiers B and C are on the same slope, but are going in opposite directions.

- Skiers C and D are going in the same direction, but C is going uphill while D is going downhill.

- The slopes are equally steep at B, C and D.

- The mathematical definition of gradient is based upon the convention that one is moving from left to right. If the snow-slope were a mathematical graph, then the gradients at A, B, C and D would be zero, positive, positive and negative, respectively.

2.3 Gradient graphs

> (a) Explain why D is not a stationary point.
>
> (b) Why do you think the word **local** is used for the maximum and minimum points above?

(a) The graph is not locally straight at D and its gradient at D is therefore undefined. (At a stationary point the gradient must be zero.)

(b) At a **local** maximum the curve is higher than at **nearby** points but not necessarily higher than at all other points on the curve.

Infinitely many points on this curve are higher than the local maximum and infinitely many are lower than the local minimum.

2.5 Finding gradients numerically

> Why does this give only an approximation?
>
> How could you obtain a better approximation to the actual gradient?
>
> Obtain a value for the gradient using a calculator or computer. Details are given on technology datasheet: *Calculating gradients*.

When $u = 3.1$ then $v = u^2 = 9.61$ and the gradient at $(3, 9)$ is approximately

$$\frac{9.61 - 9}{3.1 - 3} = 6.1$$

This is only approximate because you are using points on the **curve** and not on the tangent.

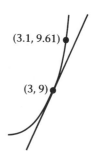

(3.1, 9.61)

(3, 9)

To obtain a better approximation, use a value of u closer to 3, for example $u = 3.01$. This is equivalent to zooming in closer. The approximation then becomes

$$\frac{9.0601 - 9}{3.01 - 3} = 6.01$$

You can program a microcomputer to perform these repetitive calculations with accuracy and speed. As u tends to 3, the value obtained for the gradient tends to 6.

Zoom!

1　With increasing magnification, the curve looks more and more like a straight line.

2　You should expect to see the curve looking more and more like a horizontal straight line.

3　When you zoom into the cubic graph at $(4, -9)$ the curve looks more and more like a horizontal straight line.

Zooming in at $x = \frac{2}{3}$ also leads to a horizontal line.

4　(a) $y = |x|$ is locally straight near all values of x, except $x = 0$.

　(b) $y = 100x^2$ is locally straight everywhere.

　(c) $y = \text{Int}\,(x)$ is locally straight near any value of x which is **not** an integer but has a discontinuity at each integer value.

　(d) $y = |x^2 - 4|$ is locally straight near all values of x, except $x = \pm 2$.

5E　(a) $y = \frac{1}{5}\sin 3x$ has $\frac{1}{5}$ of the amplitude (y stretch; scale factor $\frac{1}{5}$) and oscillates three times as frequently (x stretch, scale factor $\frac{1}{3}$) as $y = \sin x$.

　(b) Both graphs look like the graph of $y = \sin x$ with 'wrinkles'. When magnified the wrinkles become more obvious.

　(c) $y = \sin x + \frac{1}{1000}\sin 1000x$ or any similar function.

Measuring gradients

Your results for the gradients may vary slightly from the answers given here because of inaccuracies when using the gradient measurer.

1 (a) 1.5   (b) (i) 1   (ii) 2   (iii) 3

(c) −2   (d) (i) −1   (ii) −3

(e)

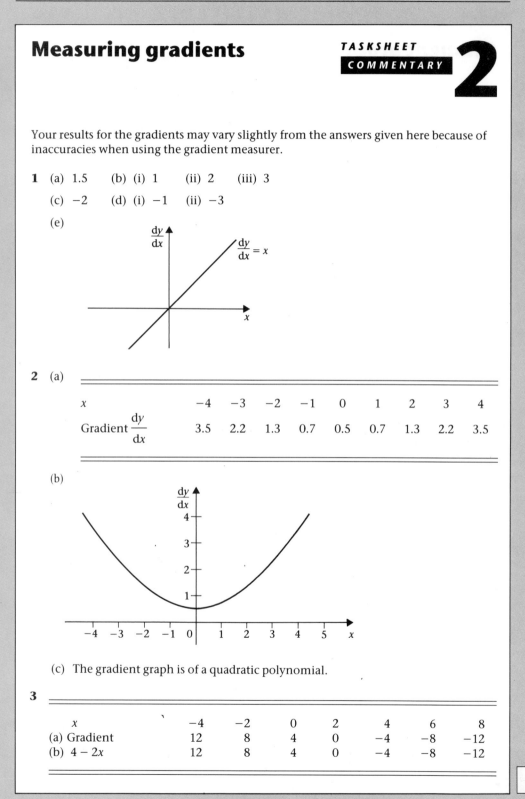

2 (a)

x	−4	−3	−2	−1	0	1	2	3	4
Gradient $\dfrac{dy}{dx}$	3.5	2.2	1.3	0.7	0.5	0.7	1.3	2.2	3.5

(b)

(c) The gradient graph is of a quadratic polynomial.

3

x	−4	−2	0	2	4	6	8
(a) Gradient	12	8	4	0	−4	−8	−12
(b) $4 - 2x$	12	8	4	0	−4	−8	−12

9

Gradient graphs

1 Any points where the tangent to the curve is horizontal correspond to a point where the gradient graph meets the *x*-axis.

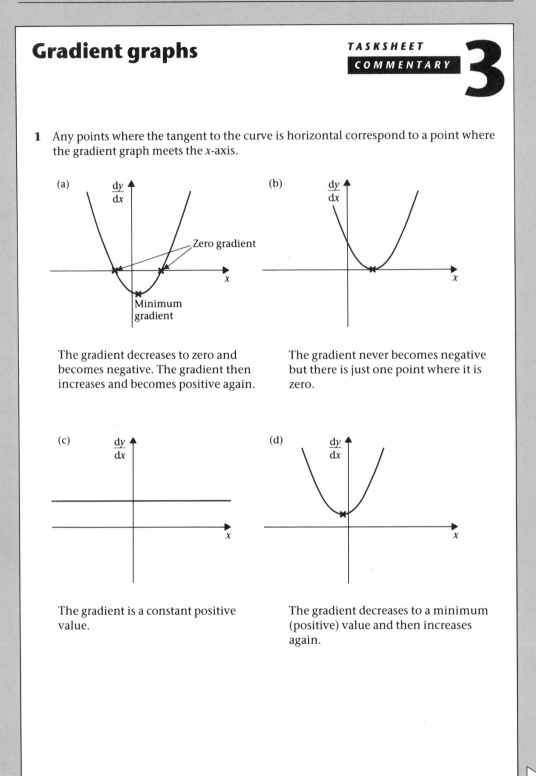

(a)

Zero gradient

Minimum gradient

The gradient decreases to zero and becomes negative. The gradient then increases and becomes positive again.

(b)

The gradient never becomes negative but there is just one point where it is zero.

(c)

The gradient is a constant positive value.

(d)

The gradient decreases to a minimum (positive) value and then increases again.

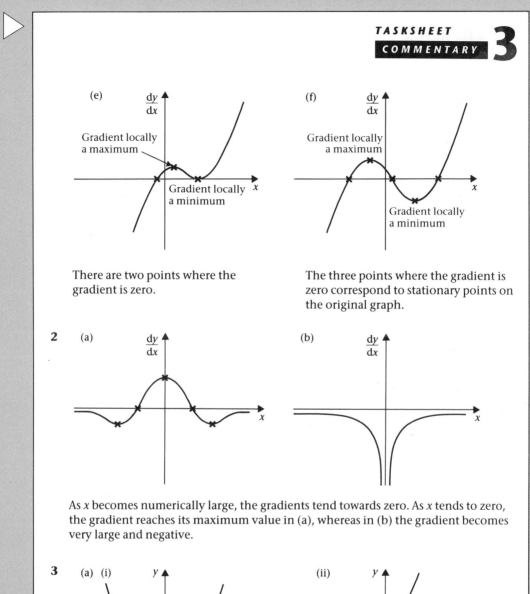

(e)

Gradient locally a maximum

Gradient locally a minimum

There are two points where the gradient is zero.

(f)

Gradient locally a maximum

Gradient locally a minimum

The three points where the gradient is zero correspond to stationary points on the original graph.

2 (a)

(b)

As x becomes numerically large, the gradients tend towards zero. As x tends to zero, the gradient reaches its maximum value in (a), whereas in (b) the gradient becomes very large and negative.

3 (a) (i)

(ii)

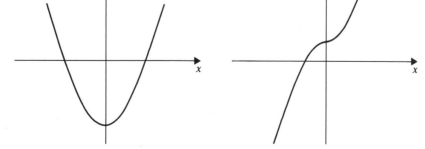

(b) There are infinitely many possible original graphs – formed by translating the graphs above parallel to the y-axis.

Quadratics

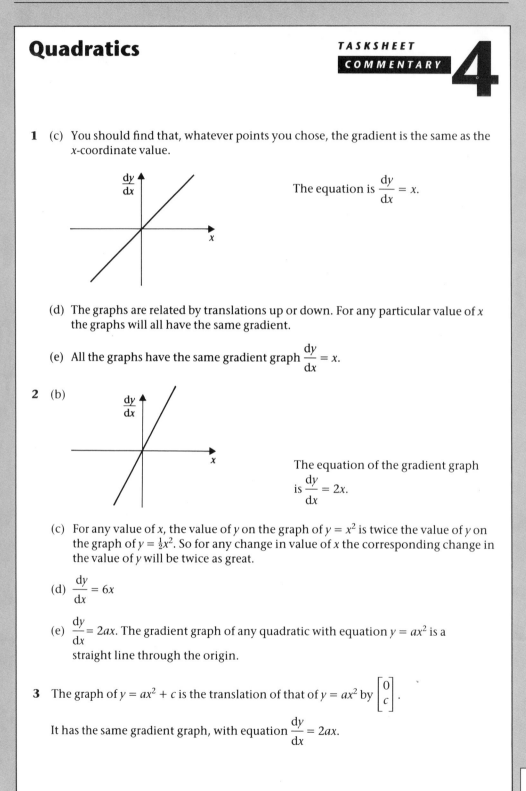

1 (c) You should find that, whatever points you chose, the gradient is the same as the *x*-coordinate value.

The equation is $\dfrac{dy}{dx} = x$.

(d) The graphs are related by translations up or down. For any particular value of *x* the graphs will all have the same gradient.

(e) All the graphs have the same gradient graph $\dfrac{dy}{dx} = x$.

2 (b)

The equation of the gradient graph is $\dfrac{dy}{dx} = 2x$.

(c) For any value of *x*, the value of *y* on the graph of $y = x^2$ is twice the value of *y* on the graph of $y = \frac{1}{2}x^2$. So for any change in value of *x* the corresponding change in the value of *y* will be twice as great.

(d) $\dfrac{dy}{dx} = 6x$

(e) $\dfrac{dy}{dx} = 2ax$. The gradient graph of any quadratic with equation $y = ax^2$ is a straight line through the origin.

3 The graph of $y = ax^2 + c$ is the translation of that of $y = ax^2$ by $\begin{bmatrix} 0 \\ c \end{bmatrix}$.

It has the same gradient graph, with equation $\dfrac{dy}{dx} = 2ax$.

Gradient functions

1 (a)

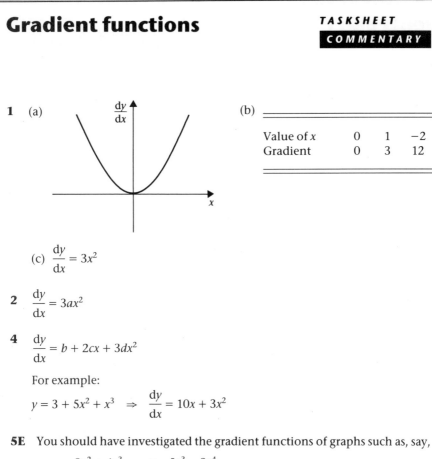

(b)

Value of x	0	1	-2	3
Gradient	0	3	12	27

(c) $\dfrac{dy}{dx} = 3x^2$

2 $\dfrac{dy}{dx} = 3ax^2$

4 $\dfrac{dy}{dx} = b + 2cx + 3dx^2$

For example:

$$y = 3 + 5x^2 + x^3 \ \Rightarrow\ \frac{dy}{dx} = 10x + 3x^2$$

5E You should have investigated the gradient functions of graphs such as, say,

$$y = 3x^2 + 4x^3, \qquad y = 5x^3 - 3x^4$$

The general conclusion you should have reached is that, if a and b are constants,

$$y = ax^n + bx^m \ \Rightarrow\ \frac{dy}{dx} = anx^{n-1} + bmx^{m-1}$$

The gradient of the sum is the sum of the gradients.

Tangents and normals

1 The normal line has gradient $-\dfrac{1}{g}$.

2 (a)

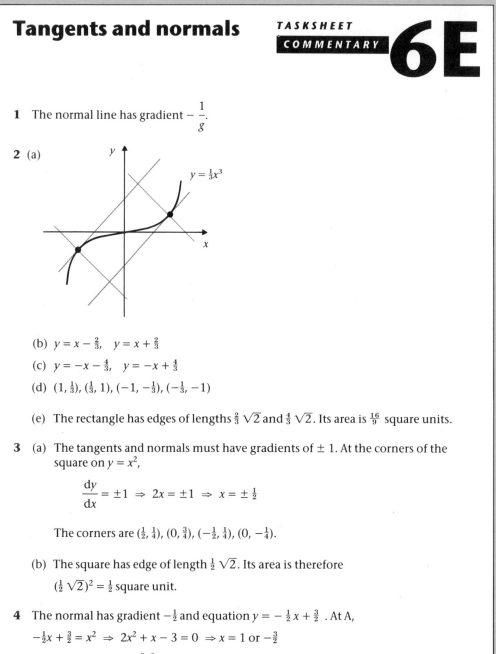

$y = \tfrac{1}{3}x^3$

(b) $y = x - \tfrac{2}{3}, \quad y = x + \tfrac{2}{3}$

(c) $y = -x - \tfrac{4}{3}, \quad y = -x + \tfrac{4}{3}$

(d) $(1, \tfrac{1}{3})$, $(\tfrac{1}{3}, 1)$, $(-1, -\tfrac{1}{3})$, $(-\tfrac{1}{3}, -1)$

(e) The rectangle has edges of lengths $\tfrac{2}{3}\sqrt{2}$ and $\tfrac{4}{3}\sqrt{2}$. Its area is $\tfrac{16}{9}$ square units.

3 (a) The tangents and normals must have gradients of ± 1. At the corners of the square on $y = x^2$,

$$\frac{\mathrm{d}y}{\mathrm{d}x} = \pm 1 \;\Rightarrow\; 2x = \pm 1 \;\Rightarrow\; x = \pm \tfrac{1}{2}$$

The corners are $(\tfrac{1}{2}, \tfrac{1}{4})$, $(0, \tfrac{3}{4})$, $(-\tfrac{1}{2}, \tfrac{1}{4})$, $(0, -\tfrac{1}{4})$.

(b) The square has edge of length $\tfrac{1}{2}\sqrt{2}$. Its area is therefore

$$(\tfrac{1}{2}\sqrt{2})^2 = \tfrac{1}{2} \text{ square unit.}$$

4 The normal has gradient $-\tfrac{1}{2}$ and equation $y = -\tfrac{1}{2}x + \tfrac{3}{2}$. At A,

$-\tfrac{1}{2}x + \tfrac{3}{2} = x^2 \;\Rightarrow\; 2x^2 + x - 3 = 0 \;\Rightarrow x = 1 \text{ or } -\tfrac{3}{2}$

A has coordinates $(-\tfrac{3}{2}, \tfrac{9}{4})$.

3 Optimisation

3.1 Graphs and gradient graphs

> (a) Explain how the details of the graph shown above are obtained.
>
> (b) What features of the $\left(x, \dfrac{dy}{dx} \right)$ gradient graph as sketched below can you relate to the shape of the (x, y) graph?
>
> (c) How are the gaps completed for this graph? How can you be certain that your sketch is roughly correct?

The graph is of $y = x^3 - 2x^2 + x + 1$.

(a) For large positive and negative values of x, the graph has a shape similar to $y = x^3$.
When x is small, the graph has a shape similar to $y = x + 1$.

(b) The zeros of the $\left(x, \dfrac{dy}{dx} \right)$ graph correspond to the

x-coordinates of the two stationary points.

The value of $\dfrac{dy}{dx}$ is negative between the two zeros,

corresponding to the negative gradient of the graph between the two stationary points. Elsewhere the gradient is positive.

(c)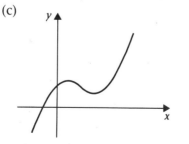

The cubic graph has at most two stationary points.

Consideration of the gradient graph confirms the general shape of the (x, y) graph. Final confirmation would come from calculating the positions of the two stationary points.

3.3 Maxima and minima

Construct a formula for the volume V in terms of a chosen variable.

Use calculus to find the maximum volume.

What simplifying assumptions have you made in obtaining your answer? How reasonable are these assumptions?

Consider a circle of paper of fixed radius R, folded at radius r. The paper folds up to a form a cylinder, of volume V.

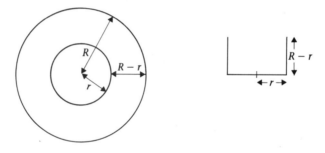

volume = area of base × height
$$V = \pi r^2(R - r)$$
$$= \pi R r^2 - \pi r^3$$
$$\frac{dV}{dr} = 2\pi Rr - 3\pi r^2 \quad \text{(Note that } R \text{ is fixed and does not vary with } r.\text{)}$$
$$= \pi r(2R - 3r)$$

$\frac{dV}{dr} = 0$ when $r = 0$ (zero volume) and when $r = \frac{2}{3}R$ (maximum

volume). The maximum volume is therefore

$$\pi \left(\tfrac{2}{3}R\right)^2 (R - \tfrac{2}{3}R) = \tfrac{4}{27}\pi R^3$$

V can, of course, be expressed in terms of other lengths, for example fixed diameter D and variable height h. It could also be expressed in terms of an area, such as the area of the base of the cake case. It is important to choose quantities which make the calculations reasonably easy. Can you find quantities for which the calculations are easier than those given above?

The main assumption that has been made is that a circular piece of paper will fold up to form a cylinder. It will in fact only do this if the sides are fluted, which then means that applying the formula for the volume of a cylinder will not give a correct expression for the volume of the cake case. The error, however, will not be very great. You might like to estimate the error.

Another assumption that has been made is that cake cases are cylindrical, when in fact most cake cases have sloping rather than vertical sides. For this discussion point, it might be helpful to get hold of some actual cake cases!

3.4 **Graphical optimisation**

> Intuitively, do you think that the amount of water which the gutter is able to carry can be increased by splaying its sides?
>
> Find an expression for the cross-sectional area of the splay-sided gutter in terms of some chosen variable quantity. Use a graph plotter to check if your intuition was correct.

Intuition alone is probably inadequate to answer the question.

Two possible ways of expressing the cross-sectional area in terms of a variable are given below, but several others are possible.

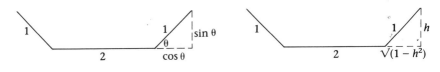

$A = (2 + \cos \theta) \sin \theta$

$A = (2 + \sqrt{1 - h^2}) h$

Whichever way is chosen should lead to a maximum value for A when the shape is as shown.

Graph sketching

1

The local maxima and minima consist of the three points marked with dots.

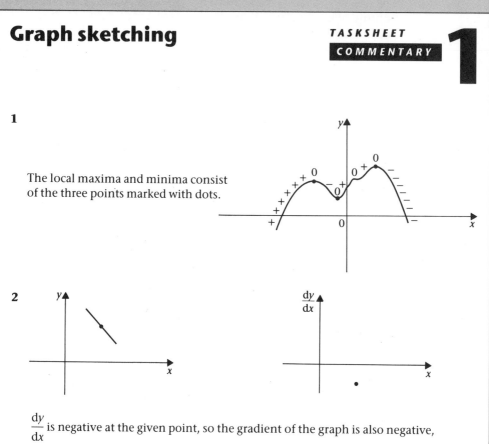

2

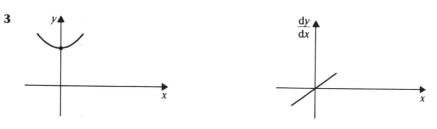

$\dfrac{dy}{dx}$ is negative at the given point, so the gradient of the graph is also negative, as shown.

3

As x increases through $x = 0$, $\dfrac{dy}{dx}$ changes from negative to positive, actually becoming zero at $x = 0$.

Since the gradient of the graph is negative for $x < 0$ and positive for $x > 0$, there is a minimum on the graph at $x = 0$.

4 A **local** maximum or minimum is the greatest or least value on the graph for a small range of values of x, in which the graph has a peak or trough. At a local maximum the gradient changes from positive to negative. At a local minimum the gradient changes from negative to positive.

Stationary points

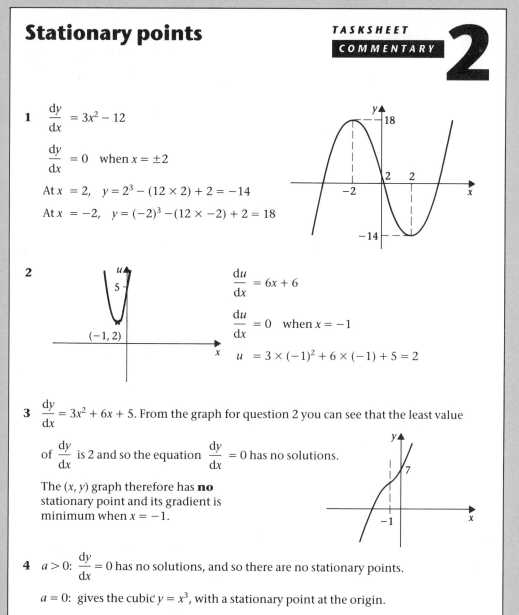

1 $\dfrac{dy}{dx} = 3x^2 - 12$

$\dfrac{dy}{dx} = 0$ when $x = \pm 2$

At $x = 2$, $y = 2^3 - (12 \times 2) + 2 = -14$

At $x = -2$, $y = (-2)^3 - (12 \times -2) + 2 = 18$

2

$\dfrac{du}{dx} = 6x + 6$

$\dfrac{du}{dx} = 0$ when $x = -1$

$u = 3 \times (-1)^2 + 6 \times (-1) + 5 = 2$

3 $\dfrac{dy}{dx} = 3x^2 + 6x + 5$. From the graph for question 2 you can see that the least value

of $\dfrac{dy}{dx}$ is 2 and so the equation $\dfrac{dy}{dx} = 0$ has no solutions.

The (x, y) graph therefore has **no**
stationary point and its gradient is
minimum when $x = -1$.

4 $a > 0$: $\dfrac{dy}{dx} = 0$ has no solutions, and so there are no stationary points.

$a = 0$: gives the cubic $y = x^3$, with a stationary point at the origin.

$a < 0$: $\dfrac{dy}{dx} = 0$ has two solutions, $x = \pm\sqrt{(-\tfrac{1}{3}a)}$, and so there are two
stationary points.

Using stationary points

1 $P = 5 + 30r - 15r^2 = 5(1 + 6r - 3r^2)$

(a) 5000 people per square kilometre. (Note: putting $r = 0$ is an idealisation; there has to be a small radius for there to be space in which people may live.)

(b) Not valid for $r > 2.15$ since $P < 0$ is meaningless.

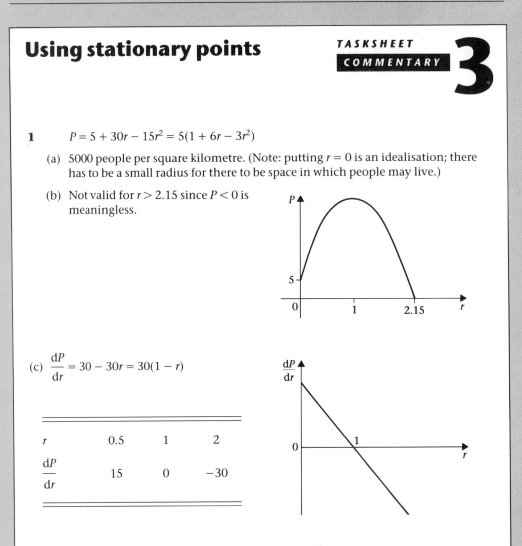

(c) $\dfrac{dP}{dr} = 30 - 30r = 30(1 - r)$

r	0.5	1	2
$\dfrac{dP}{dr}$	15	0	−30

(d) The population density rises to a maximum of 20000 people per square kilometre at a distance of 1 km from the city centre.

The population density then decreases as you go further out from the centre.

The $\left(r, \dfrac{dP}{dr} \right)$ graph shows that the maximum value of P corresponds to the value of r where $\dfrac{dP}{dr} = 0$.

For $r < 1$, the population density increases with r.

For $r > 1$, it decreases with r.

(e) 1 km from the centre. When $r = 1$, $\dfrac{dP}{dr} = 0$.

2 Let

$$y = x + \frac{10}{x}$$

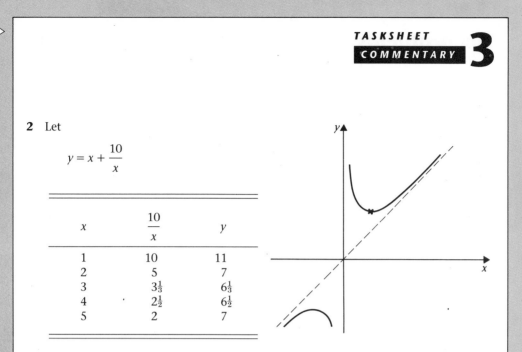

x	$\dfrac{10}{x}$	y
1	10	11
2	5	7
3	$3\frac{1}{3}$	$6\frac{1}{3}$
4	$2\frac{1}{2}$	$6\frac{1}{2}$
5	2	7

If integers only are permitted, the minimum is 7 when the numbers are 2 and 5.

If all positive numbers are permitted, the minimum is approximately 6.3, when both numbers are just less than 3.2.

If negative numbers are permitted, there is no limit to the minimum value that the sum takes.

Box problems

1 (a) The length of the net is $w + l + w + l = 100$.

$$2l + 2w = 100$$
$$l + w = 50$$
$$l = 50 - w$$

(b) The width of the net is $\frac{1}{2}w + h + \frac{1}{2}w = 40$.

$$h + w = 40$$
$$h = 40 - w$$

(c) $V = whl$
$$V = w(40 - w)(50 - w)$$

(d)

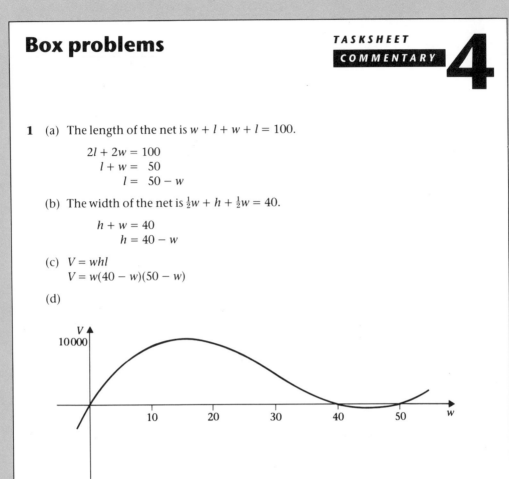

The maximum volume (of approximately $13\,130\,\text{cm}^3$) occurs when $w \approx 14.7$. The dimensions are then approximately $14.7\,\text{cm}$ by $35.3\,\text{cm}$ by $25.3\,\text{cm}$.

Note: the minimum value has no physical meaning.

2 (a) The dimensions of the box are:

length $= 6 - 2x$, width $= 4 - 2x$, height $= x$

so the volume is

$$V = (4 - 2x)(6 - 2x)x$$

(b) By sketching a graph, you will find that V is maximum when $x \approx 0.8$.

The approximate dimensions are $0.8\,\text{cm}$ by $2.4\,\text{cm}$ by $4.4\,\text{cm}$.

Optimisation

1 (a) If $x > 5$ or $x < -5$, then the base of the cone lies outside the sphere and the design constraint has been violated.

x must be smaller than the radius of the sphere if the cone is to be inside it.

(b) The diagrams indicate that the volume increases to a maximum value, then gets smaller again.

(c)

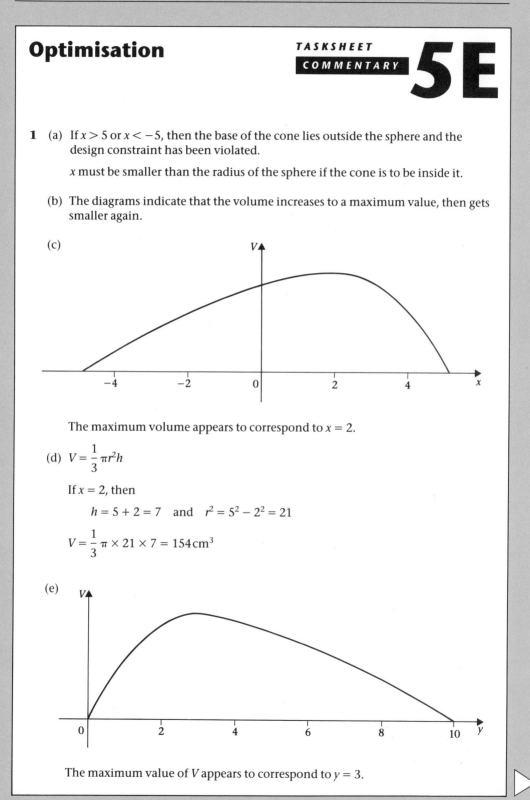

The maximum volume appears to correspond to $x = 2$.

(d) $V = \dfrac{1}{3}\pi r^2 h$

If $x = 2$, then

$$h = 5 + 2 = 7 \quad \text{and} \quad r^2 = 5^2 - 2^2 = 21$$

$$V = \frac{1}{3}\pi \times 21 \times 7 = 154 \, \text{cm}^3$$

(e)

The maximum value of V appears to correspond to $y = 3$.

(f) $V = \dfrac{1}{3}\pi(5^2 - x^2)(5 + x) = \dfrac{1}{3}\pi(5 - x)(5 + x)^2$

Writing the equation in this form makes the graph easier to sketch.

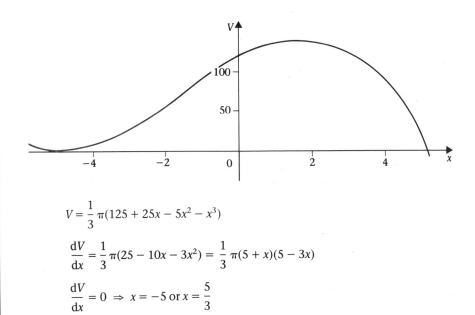

$V = \dfrac{1}{3}\pi(125 + 25x - 5x^2 - x^3)$

$\dfrac{dV}{dx} = \dfrac{1}{3}\pi(25 - 10x - 3x^2) = \dfrac{1}{3}\pi(5 + x)(5 - 3x)$

$\dfrac{dV}{dx} = 0 \;\Rightarrow\; x = -5 \text{ or } x = \dfrac{5}{3}$

The minimum is at $(-5, 0)$. The maximum is at $(1.67, 155.1)$.

The maximum volume is $155\,\text{cm}^3$.

(g) Using y as the variable, the height of the cone $h = 10 - y$ and the radius is given by $r^2 = 5^2 - (5 - y)^2$.

$V = \dfrac{1}{3}\pi\{5^2 - (5 - y)^2\}(10 - y) = \dfrac{1}{3}\pi(y^3 - 20y^2 + 100y)$

$\dfrac{dV}{dy} = \dfrac{1}{3}\pi(3y^2 - 40y + 100) = \dfrac{1}{3}\pi(3y - 10)(y - 10)$

$\dfrac{dV}{dy} = 0 \;\Rightarrow\; y = \dfrac{10}{3} \text{ or } y = 10$

The minimum is at $(10, 0)$. The maximum is at $(3.33, 155.1)$.

Note: $1.67 + 3.33 = 5.00$, as would be expected.

(h)

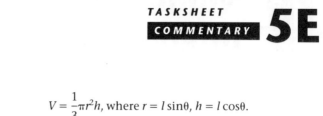

$V = \dfrac{1}{3}\pi r^2 h$, where $r = l\sin\theta$, $h = l\cos\theta$.

Hence

$$V = \frac{1}{3}\pi l^3 \sin^2\theta \cos\theta$$

In finding this expression you have introduced a new variable, the slant height l. This must be eliminated from the expression for V, so that the expression for V is in terms of θ only. This can be done easily by substituting $l = 10\cos\theta$.

This result follows directly from the well-known geometrical result that the angle subtended on a diameter is a right-angle.

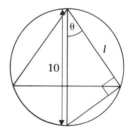

So you have

$$V = \frac{1}{3}\pi 1000 \cos^4\theta \sin^2\theta$$

which is a maximum when $\theta = 35.3°$, giving a volume of 155.1 cm³.

2   Let the price per bike be £P. The number sold drops by 40 for each increase of £1 in the price, and so the number sold is

   $5000 - 40(P - 100) = 9000 - 40P$

   total revenue = £$(9000 - 40P)P$
   total costs = £$50000 + 85(9000 - 40P)$
   profit = revenue − costs = £$(-815000 + 12400P - 40P^2)$

   $\dfrac{\text{d (Profit)}}{\text{d}P} = 0$ when $12400 - 80P = 0$,   i.e. $P = 155$

number sold = $9000 - 40P = 2800$

Approximately 2800 should be manufactured and they should be sold at a price of £155 each.

4 Numerical integration

4.1 Areas under graphs

> What total volume of water flows from the tap in 20 minutes?
>
> How is this amount represented on the graph?

Water flows at a constant 15 litres per minute for 20 minutes. The total volume of water is $15 \times 20 = 300$ litres.

This is represented by the area of the rectangle (shaded on the graph).

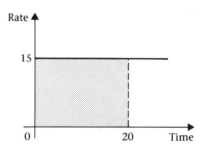

4.3 Integration

> Consider the function $y = \sqrt{(4 - x^2)}$.
>
> (a) Draw a diagram to illustrate the area represented by
>
> $$\int_0^2 \sqrt{(4 - x^2)} \, dx$$
>
> (b) What is the precise value of this integral?
>
> (c) Use the mid-ordinate rule with two strips to estimate this integral.

(a)

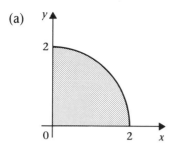

The shaded area under the graph of $y = \sqrt{(4 - x^2)}$ is one quarter of the area of the circle with equation $x^2 + y^2 = 4$. The radius is 2.

(b) The area of the circle is 4π. So $\displaystyle\int_0^2 \sqrt{(4 - x^2)}\, dx = \pi$.

(c) $\displaystyle\int_0^2 \sqrt{(4 - x^2)}\, dx \approx (1 \times 1.936) + (1 \times 1.323) \approx 3.26$

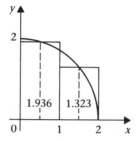

4.4 Numerical methods

What are the values of:

(a) the width, h, of each strip;

(b) x_1, y_1, x_2, y_2;

(c) the areas of strips ① and ②;

(d) x_7, y_7 and the area of strip ⑦?

(a) $h = \frac{2}{10} = 0.2$

(b) $x_1 = 0.1,\quad y_1 \approx 1.997,\quad x_2 = 0.3,\quad y_2 \approx 1.977$

(c) $0.2 \times y_1 \approx 0.399,\quad 0.2 \times y_2 \approx 0.395$

(d) $x_7 = 0.1 + 6 \times 0.2 = 1.3,\quad y_7 \approx 1.520,\quad 0.2 \times y_7 \approx 0.304$

4.5 Negative areas

(a) Use the data represented above to estimate the total trade balance from 1979 to 1987.

(b) Using a numerical method, evaluate the integral

$$\int_a^b (3x^2 - 18x + 24)\, dx$$

for intervals given by

$$a = 1, b = 2; \quad a = 2, b = 4; \quad a = 1, b = 4.$$

Comment on the calculations above with reference to the graph given below.

(a) Total balance $\approx -0.6 + 3 + 6.6 + 4.5 + 2.7 + 2 + 3.2 + 0.1 - 1.5$
thousand million pounds
$\approx$ £20000 million

(b) The integrals are $4, -4, 0$ respectively.

In the first case, the area is entirely above the x-axis. In the second, it is entirely below. In the third, the areas above and below the x-axis are equal and cancel each other out.

Areas

1

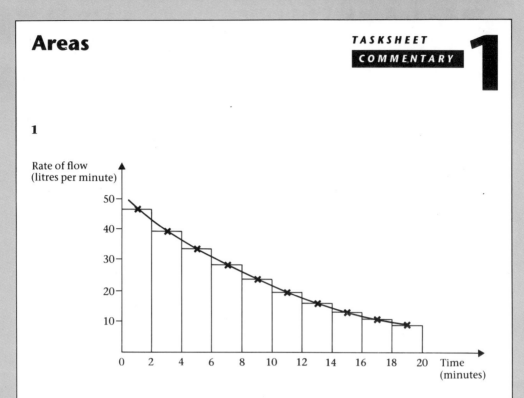

The given rates of flow are decreasing fairly steadily, so it seems likely that in each two-minute interval ($0 \rightarrow 2$, $2 \rightarrow 4$, $4 \rightarrow 6$, . . .) the rate is falling steadily too.

With this assumption, the rate of flow at the middle of each interval enables you to give a reasonable estimate of the volume of water flowing during the interval.

(a) The estimate of the total volume drained during the 20 minutes then corresponds to the area under the steps shown on the graph,

$$2 \times (46.3 + 39.7 + 34.0 + \ldots + 11.6) \approx 510$$

The volume is about 510 litres.

(b) The main assumption is that the rate of flow at the middle of each interval is a good estimate for the **average** rate of flow during the interval.

(c) The explanation is given below the diagram and in part (a).

TASKSHEET COMMENTARY 1

2

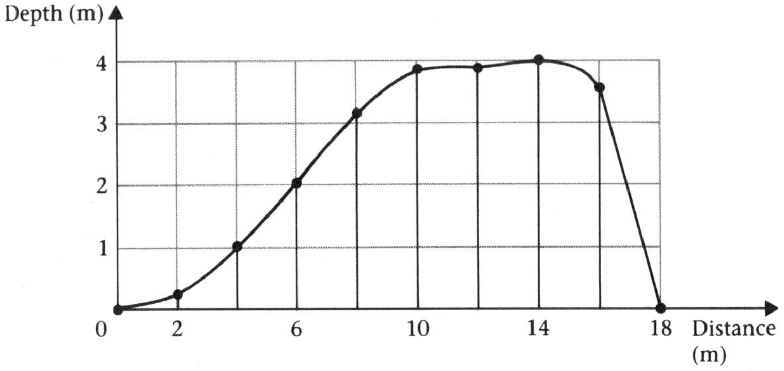

You can plot on a graph the points corresponding to the given depths and then draw a smooth curve through them. It is probable that this curve will give a good estimate of the depth of the river at intermediate points. In fact the graph is a sketch of a cross-section of the river, reflected in the horizontal axis.

To estimate the area under the graph, you can use one of the following methods:

- counting squares;
- joining the given points with straight lines and calculating areas of trapezia;
- using rectangles to approximate the area.

The area is about 43 m^2.

Methods of estimation

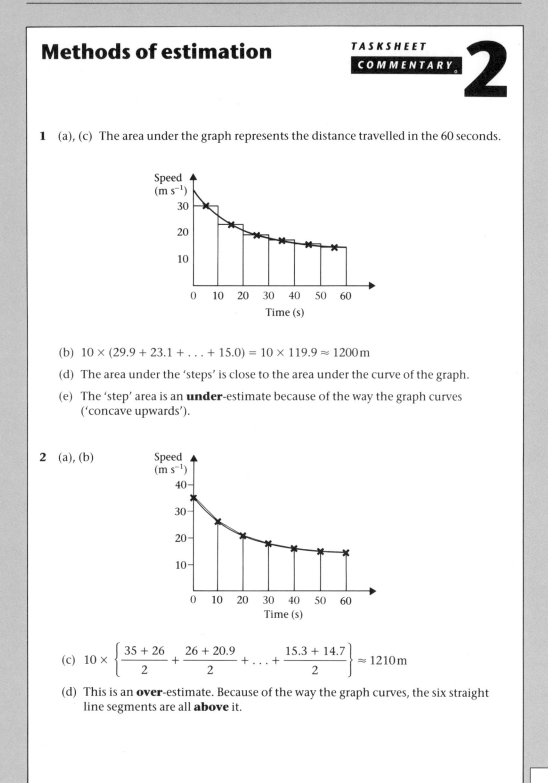

1 (a), (c) The area under the graph represents the distance travelled in the 60 seconds.

(b) $10 \times (29.9 + 23.1 + \ldots + 15.0) = 10 \times 119.9 \approx 1200\,\text{m}$

(d) The area under the 'steps' is close to the area under the curve of the graph.

(e) The 'step' area is an **under**-estimate because of the way the graph curves ('concave upwards').

2 (a), (b)

(c) $10 \times \left\{ \dfrac{35 + 26}{2} + \dfrac{26 + 20.9}{2} + \ldots + \dfrac{15.3 + 14.7}{2} \right\} \approx 1210\,\text{m}$

(d) This is an **over**-estimate. Because of the way the graph curves, the six straight line segments are all **above** it.

To the limit

1 (a) $h = \dfrac{b - a}{n}$

(b) $x_1 = a + \dfrac{h}{2}$

(c) x is increased by h each time.

2 (a) (i) 3.15241 (ii) 3.14543 (iii) 3.14295 (iv) 3.14207

$\pi \approx 3.14159$. The error is approximately divided by 3 each time the number of strips is doubled.

(b) Hundreds of strips would be needed – the mid-ordinate rule estimates are converging very slowly to the true value. This is not a sensible method of estimating π to 4 decimal places.

3 (a) $h = 0.2$; $x_0 = 0, x_1 = 0.2$; $y_0 = 2, y_1 \approx 1.990$; area ≈ 0.399

(b) $x_6 = 0.2 \times 6 = 1.2, x_7 = 1.4$; $y_6 = 1.6, y_7 \approx 1.428$

The average height of the 7th strip is 1.514, so the area is approximately 0.303.

4 (a) (i) 3.10452 (ii) 3.12847 (iii) 3.13695 (iv) 3.13995

The trapezium rule under-estimates π (by more than the corresponding mid-ordinate rule over-estimates π). Again, the errors are approximately divided by 3 each time the number of strips is doubled.

(b) This method is also not a sensible one for estimating π to 4 decimal places.

'Negative' areas

1 (a) (i) 242 (ii) 44 (iii) −64

(b) $u = 11$

2 $\int_0^5 x \, dx = 12.5$

The mid-ordinate estimates should be approximately

$$\int_4^5 (x^2 - 4x) \, dx \approx 2.3$$

So $\int_0^4 (x^2 - 4x) \, dx \approx -10.6$

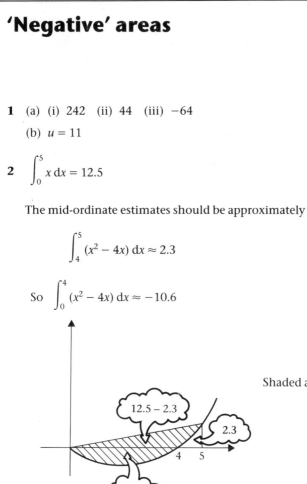

Shaded area $\approx (12.5 - 2.3) + 10.6$
≈ 21 square units

12.5 − 2.3

2.3

10.6

3

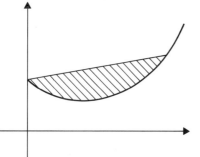

$$\int_0^5 (x + 5) \, dx = \left(\frac{5 + 10}{2} \right) \times 5 = 37.5$$

$$\int_0^5 (x^2 - 4x + 5) \, dx \approx 16.7$$

Shaded area $\approx 37.5 - 16.7$
≈ 21 square units

This confirms the value obtained in question 2.

Traffic

1 $\int_0^{10} \frac{t(20 - t)}{5} \, dt \approx 133$

Car A travels about 133 m during the 10 seconds in which it accelerates from rest.

2 During these 10 seconds, car B will travel $20 \times 10 = 200$ m. So car B must be at least 67 m from car A at the start if it is to avoid slowing down.

(In practice; rather more than 67 m will be required since it would be dangerous for the cars to get very close to each other. The actual length of the cars has not been considered, nor has the fact that A initially has to travel around a bend.)

3 If the traffic is moving at $20 \, \text{m s}^{-1}$, then in one hour the length of traffic passing is $20 \times 3600 = 72\,000$ m.

The average space between cars is $\frac{72\,000}{1200} = 60$ m.

So car A is unlikely to find a gap of sufficient length if the traffic is evenly spaced. The traffic is very unlikely to be evenly spaced and so A is likely to find a gap without having to wait too long.

5 Algebraic integration

5.1 The integral function

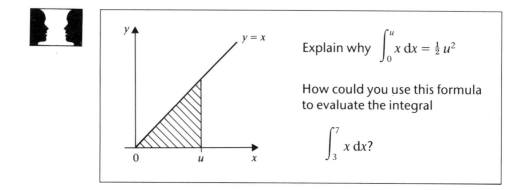

Explain why $\displaystyle\int_0^u x \, dx = \tfrac{1}{2}u^2$

How could you use this formula to evaluate the integral

$$\int_3^7 x \, dx?$$

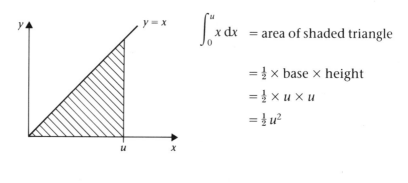

$\displaystyle\int_0^u x \, dx$ = area of shaded triangle

$= \tfrac{1}{2} \times$ base $\times$ height

$= \tfrac{1}{2} \times u \times u$

$= \tfrac{1}{2}u^2$

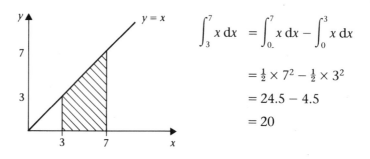

$\displaystyle\int_3^7 x \, dx = \int_{0}^7 x \, dx - \int_0^3 x \, dx$

$= \tfrac{1}{2} \times 7^2 - \tfrac{1}{2} \times 3^2$

$= 24.5 - 4.5$

$= 20$

5.2 Polynomial integrals

> What do you think the integral functions are for
>
> (a) $f(x) = x^3$ (b) $f(x) = 2x^2$ (c) $f(x) = x^2 - 3x$?
>
> Check your conjectures using the 'area' option on a graph plotter. Guidance is given on technology datasheet: *Area functions*.

(a) $f(x) = x^3 \Rightarrow A(x) = \dfrac{x^4}{4}$

(b) $f(x) = 2x^2 \Rightarrow A(x) = \dfrac{2x^3}{3}$

(c) $f(x) = x^2 - 3x \Rightarrow A(x) = \dfrac{x^3}{3} - \dfrac{3x^2}{2}$

In this discussion point there is an opportunity to become familiar with the use of the 'area' option before it is needed on tasksheet 2.

5.3 Numerical or algebraic integration?

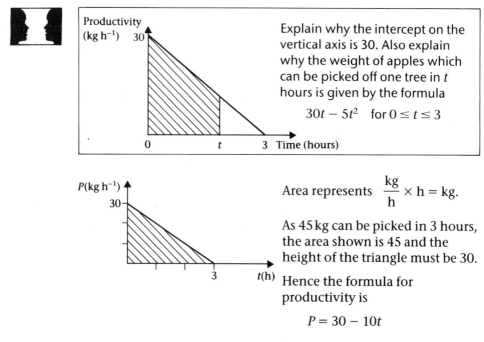

Explain why the intercept on the vertical axis is 30. Also explain why the weight of apples which can be picked off one tree in t hours is given by the formula

$$30t - 5t^2 \quad \text{for } 0 \le t \le 3$$

Area represents $\dfrac{\text{kg}}{\text{h}} \times \text{h} = \text{kg}$.

As 45 kg can be picked in 3 hours, the area shown is 45 and the height of the triangle must be 30.

Hence the formula for productivity is

$$P = 30 - 10t$$

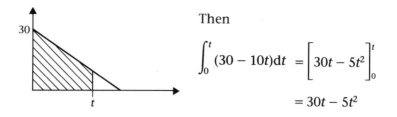

Then

$$\int_0^t (30 - 10t)dt = \left[30t - 5t^2 \right]_0^t$$

$$= 30t - 5t^2$$

5.4 The fundamental theorem of calculus

What simple relationship is there between a function and its integral function? The table below may help you to spot the connection.

If you differentiate the integral function, you obtain the function you are integrating, i.e.

$$\frac{d}{dx} (A(x)) = f(x)$$

5.5 The indefinite angle

Differentiate each of
$$x^2 + 5x + 1, \quad x^2 + 5x + 4, \quad x^2 + 5x - 3.$$

Explain why each of these functions could be used as an integral function for $2x + 5$ and why each gives the same answer for

$$\int_1^2 (2x + 5)\, dx$$

Each has derivative $2x + 5$.

According to the fundamental theorem of calculus, each can therefore be used as an integral function for $2x + 5$. Also, you should note that

$$\left[x^2 + 5x + c \right]_0^t = (14 + c) - (6 + c) = 8$$

because the c's cancel out.

Finding integral functions

1

u	0	1	2	3	4	5	6
A	0	$\frac{1}{3}$	$2\frac{2}{3}$	9	$21\frac{1}{3}$	$41\frac{2}{3}$	72

2 (a) $\displaystyle\int_2^4 x^2\,dx = \int_0^4 x^2\,dx - \int_0^2 x^2\,dx$ ⟵ $A(4) - A(2)$

$\qquad\qquad = 21\frac{1}{3} - 2\frac{2}{3}$

$\qquad\qquad = 18\frac{2}{3}$

(b) $\displaystyle\int_1^3 x^2\,dx = A(3) - A(1)$

$\qquad\qquad = 9 - \frac{1}{3}$

$\qquad\qquad = 8\frac{2}{3}$

3 (a)

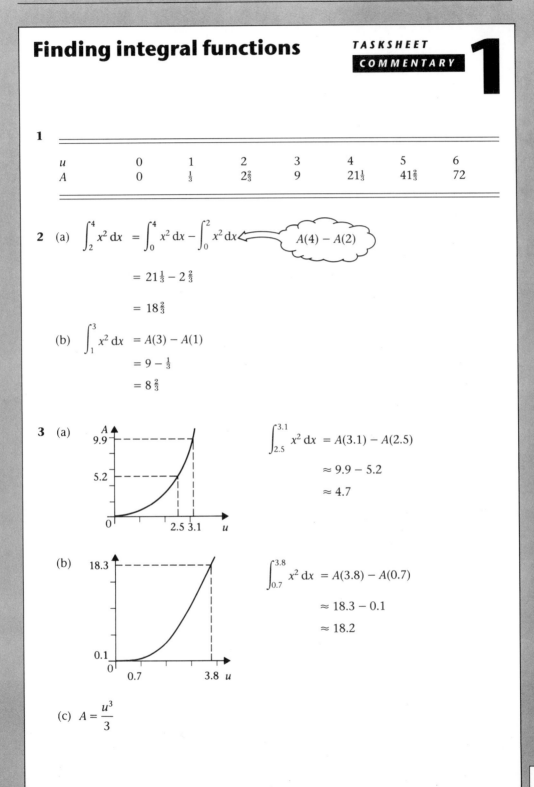

$\displaystyle\int_{2.5}^{3.1} x^2\,dx = A(3.1) - A(2.5)$

$\qquad\qquad \approx 9.9 - 5.2$

$\qquad\qquad \approx 4.7$

(b)

$\displaystyle\int_{0.7}^{3.8} x^2\,dx = A(3.8) - A(0.7)$

$\qquad\qquad \approx 18.3 - 0.1$

$\qquad\qquad \approx 18.2$

(c) $A = \dfrac{u^3}{3}$

Polynomials

1   (a), (b)

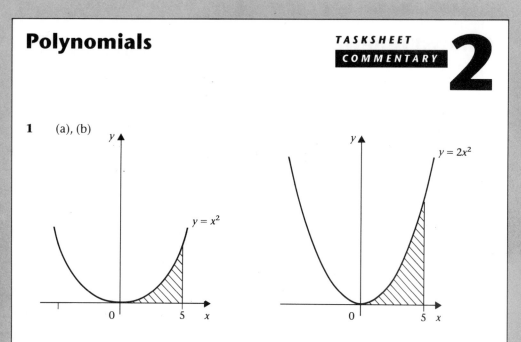

(c)   The graph of $y = 2x^2$ is obtained by a one-way stretch $\times 2$ from the y-axis. Areas are therefore increased by a factor of 2.

(d) $\displaystyle\int_a^b kx^2 \, dx = k \int_a^b x^2 \, dx$

2   (a)   (b)

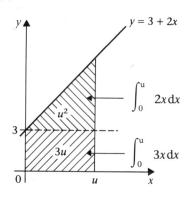

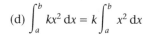

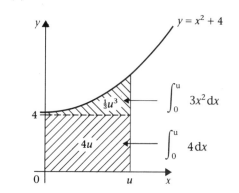

3, 4 $f(x) = ax^2 + bx + c \;\;\Rightarrow\;\; A(x) = \dfrac{ax^3}{3} + \dfrac{bx^2}{2} + cx$

5, 6 $f(x) = ax^3 + bx^2 + cx + d \;\;\Rightarrow\;\; A(x) = \dfrac{ax^4}{4} + \dfrac{bx^3}{3} + \dfrac{cx^2}{2} + dx$

Catalyst renewal

1 $\displaystyle\int_0^3 4(t-5)^2\,dt \quad = 4\int_0^3 (t^2 - 10t + 25)\,dt$

$$= 4\left[\tfrac{1}{3}t^3 - 5t^2 + 25t\right]_0^3$$

$$= 156 \ \text{(kg)}$$

2 (a) Average productivity is $\dfrac{156}{3\frac{1}{2}}$ kg per hour = 44.6 kg per hour.

(b) $\displaystyle\int_0^{1.5} 4(t-5)^2\,dt = 4\left[\tfrac{1}{3}t^3 - 5t^2 + 25t\right]_0^{1.5} = 109.5$

This is the number of kilograms produced in 2 hours, so the average productivity is 54.75 kg per hour.

(c) $\displaystyle\int_0^{\frac{2}{3}} 4(t-5)^2\,dt = 58.17$ kg produced in 1 hour 10 minutes.

Average productivity is 49.86 kg per hour.

3 If the catalyst is changed after t hours, the output in kg per hour is

$$\frac{4(\tfrac{1}{3}t^3 - 5t^2 + 25t)}{t + 0.5}\,.$$

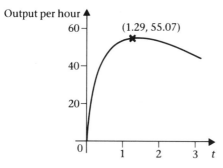

Using a graph plotter you can see that maximum output per hour is achieved when the catalyst is renewed after approximately 1.29 hours (1 hour 17 minutes), giving average productivity of 55.07 kg per hour.

4E In a $3\frac{1}{2}$ hour production cycle 156 kg are produced.

Profit in £ is $(156 \times 3) - (50 \times 3\frac{1}{2}) - 150 = £143$.

(a) Profit per kg sold = £143 ÷ 156 = £0.92.

(b) Profit per hour = $143 \div 3\frac{1}{2} = £40.86$.

5E Profit per kg is a maximum £0.94 when $t = 2.53$, i.e. the catalyst is changed after 2 hours 32 minutes.

Profit per hour is a maximum £47.13 when $t = 2.155$, i.e. the catalyst is changed after 2 hours 9 minutes.

The company should maximise profit per hour to achieve maximum profit per annum.

Straight line segments

1

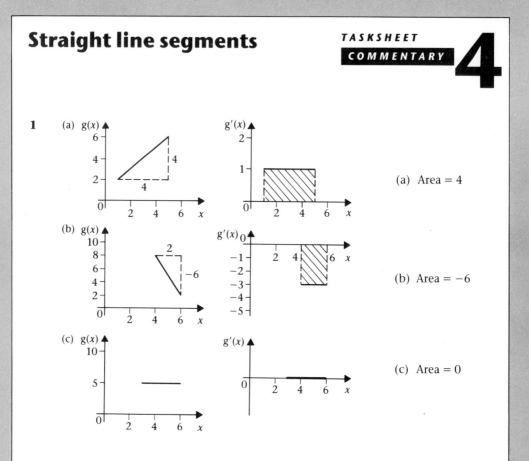

(a) Area = 4

(b) Area = −6

(c) Area = 0

The difference in the y-coordinates of the end points equals the area under the gradient graph.

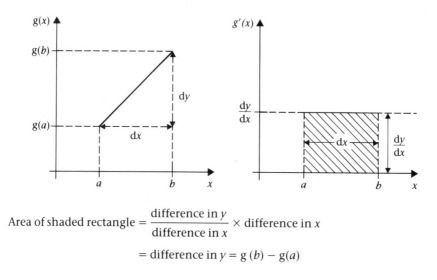

$$\text{Area of shaded rectangle} = \frac{\text{difference in } y}{\text{difference in } x} \times \text{difference in } x$$

$$= \text{difference in } y = g(b) - g(a)$$

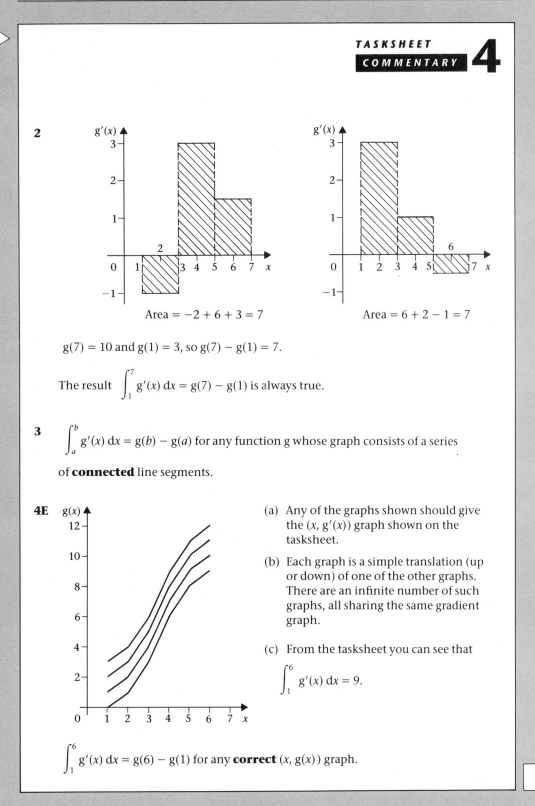

2

Area $= -2 + 6 + 3 = 7$

Area $= 6 + 2 - 1 = 7$

$g(7) = 10$ and $g(1) = 3$, so $g(7) - g(1) = 7$.

The result $\displaystyle\int_1^7 g'(x)\,dx = g(7) - g(1)$ is always true.

3 $\displaystyle\int_a^b g'(x)\,dx = g(b) - g(a)$ for any function g whose graph consists of a series

of **connected** line segments.

4E

(a) Any of the graphs shown should give the $(x, g'(x))$ graph shown on the tasksheet.

(b) Each graph is a simple translation (up or down) of one of the other graphs. There are an infinite number of such graphs, all sharing the same gradient graph.

(c) From the tasksheet you can see that

$$\int_1^6 g'(x)\,dx = 9.$$

$\displaystyle\int_1^6 g'(x)\,dx = g(6) - g(1)$ for any **correct** $(x, g(x))$ graph.

Constants of integration

1 $y = 2x + 3$ crosses the y-axis at $(0, 3)$. c is the intercept on the y-axis.

2

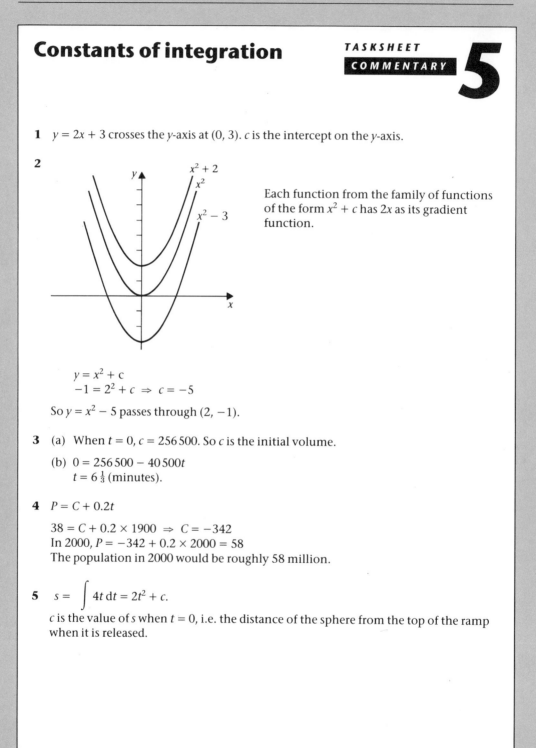

Each function from the family of functions of the form $x^2 + c$ has $2x$ as its gradient function.

$$y = x^2 + c$$
$$-1 = 2^2 + c \Rightarrow c = -5$$

So $y = x^2 - 5$ passes through $(2, -1)$.

3 (a) When $t = 0$, $c = 256\,500$. So c is the initial volume.

(b) $0 = 256\,500 - 40\,500t$
$t = 6\frac{1}{3}$ (minutes).

4 $P = C + 0.2t$

$38 = C + 0.2 \times 1900 \Rightarrow C = -342$
In 2000, $P = -342 + 0.2 \times 2000 = 58$
The population in 2000 would be roughly 58 million.

5 $s = \displaystyle\int 4t\,dt = 2t^2 + c.$

c is the value of s when $t = 0$, i.e. the distance of the sphere from the top of the ramp when it is released.

6 $c = 0.5 \Rightarrow s = 2t^2 + 0.5$
When $t = 1$, $s = 2.5$

The ramp is 2.5 m in length.

7 $s = 2t^2 + 1$
$2.5 = 2t^2 + 1 \Rightarrow t^2 = 0.75 \Rightarrow t \approx 0.866$
The sphere takes approximately 0.87 seconds to reach the bottom.

8E   The area is measured from $x = 3$.

9E   The original function is $y = 2x - 4$ and the area is measured from $x = 2$.